SCRIPTURAL BONDAGE

TERRANCE WILLIAMS

Copyright © 2015 Terrance Williams

All rights reserved.

ISBN-13: 978-1516853113

ISBN-10: 1516853113

DEDICATION

This book is dedicated to everyone. My entire family and all of my friends; this book is especially written in mindful thinking of you guys. I love you, and thanks for taking the time out to share some thoughts with me in this writing. Please don't rush through this book. There are many vital points I would want every reader to digest. Even if the thoughts are not agreed upon, be sure to finish this book with a complete understanding of what the author is and is not saying. Any questions, email me at nwillfitness850@gmail.com. Thanks!

CONTENTS

1	A Release Needed	3
2	A Clever Counterfeit	6
3	What Was Finished?	9
4	Christ; the KEY	21
5	The Gospel Chart	29
6	Psalm 18:25, 26	32
7	The Rich Man and Lazarus	49
8	Structural vs. Functional	56
9	Treasures and Vessels	63
10	Conclusive Thoughts	65
Appendix 1 – Burn Forever?		68
Appendix 2 – Picking Up Swords		78
Appendix 3 – Its Own Interpreter		80

ACKNOWLEDGMENTS

I would like to thank God for using the Truth For The Final Generation Ministry, which was the instrument to deliver me the truth of His character via books and sermon messages. Also, the late F.T. Wright, played a big role with delivering the gospel truth in two of his many books: God's Sabbath Rest and Behold Your God. My wife and mother indeed I can't forget, with their support as I continue to enter into deep theological studies; day in and day out.

Reference Abbreviations

COL = Christ Object Lessons

DA = Desire of Ages

DD = Darkness before Dawn

GC = Great Controversy

GW = Gospel Workers

PP = Patriarchs and Prophets

RH = Review and Herald

1SM = Selected Messages (Book 1)

1SP = Spirit of Prophecy (Volume 1)

9T = Testimonies (Volume 9)

5T = Testimony for the Church (Volume 5)

*All written by the late Ellen G. White

INTRO: A RELEASE NEEDED

I recall at age seven wanting to play Little League Football. My mother therefore signed me up, leaving my anticipation "higher than the sky"; until I experienced that first hit. "I don't want to play anymore" I told her. "Whatever you start, you must finish," she replied. My football career lasted 17 years, and for 17 years I was in football bondage.

We all have, or have had some sort of bondage:

- financial bondage
- career bondage
- family bondage
- mental/physical bondage
- etc.

In a world full of shackles, how can one experience freedom? The rich are seeking to become richer. The educated are acquiring higher education. The materialist are obtaining more for "secure comfort." These realities are never ending! Therefore, we are left in a continuing state of enslavement. The wise man Solomon felt this bondage and sought freedom in every way one can imagine, but concluded that "all is vanity" (Ecclesiastes 12:8).

Q: Living in such doomed reality, what hope is it? Is freedom truly an actuality or a mere facade?

In this book: thoughts will be shared, hidden truths will be found, history will be examined; on what true freedom is.

All my life I've been told that "the word of God" brings liberty; freedom to an enslaved soul. Growing up hearing this idea accustomed my mind to accept it, but never could I truly experience it. So the million dollar question is, WHY? Why couldn't I experience this freedom?

A: The "word of God," in itself, doesn't bring freedom. But "rightly dividing" the word of God, and seeing the Word (Christ) of God in the word (bible) of God brings true freedom (2nd Timothy 2:15 / 2nd Corinthians 3:1-16 / Isaiah 28:10).

The sacrifice of Christ as an atonement for sin is the great truth around which all other truths cluster. In order to be rightly understood and appreciated, every truth in the word of God, from Genesis to Revelation, must be studied in the light that streams from the cross of Calvary (GW 315.2).

Search the scriptures; for in them ye think ye have eternal life: and they are they which testify of me (John 5:39).

Q: How must we understand and appreciate the Old Testament?

- By studying Hebrew linguistics?
- By understanding Jewish traditions and culture?

A: These both and many other suggestions have their place, and I by no means condemn such reality. But notice the words of inspiration, "every truth in the word of God, from Genesis to Revelation, must be studied in the light that streams from the cross of Calvary" (GW 315.2).

The Apostle Paul comprehended this same thing:

But their minds were blinded: for until this day remaineth the same vail untaken away in the reading of the old testament; which vail is done away in Christ. But even unto this day, when Moses is read, the vail is upon their heart. **Nevertheless when it shall turn to the Lord, the vail shall be taken away** (2nd Corinth. 3:14-16).

- ➤ As we continue, remember that Christ is the Key that unlocks all mysteries.

CHAPTER 2: A CLEVER COUNTERFEIT

Q: Who was, or is, the biggest student of the word of God?

Some may say:

1. **_Antediluvians_** - although during a time of oral communication, the people before the flood, knew well of the oracles of God. Considering the average life span, 500- 800 years, for one to fathom a child of God during that time to be the biggest student of the word of God holds some strength.
2. **_Jesus_** - the eternal Word of God. *God's thought made audible (DA 19.2).* Christ, although the Son of God, never used His divinity to have an advantage with overcoming sin as a man. *Only **by** the word could He (Christ) resist temptation* (DA 123.5). I will agree that Christ appropriated the word, where it was manifested in His character like no other. But the emphasis here will be on a creature who is not at one (as Christ was) with the

word, but who, by far, spent/spends the most time in the word of God.

Q: Who is this creature?

A: Satan

We're told that "Satan is a diligent Bible student" (9T 16.1).

- 2,500 years (oral communication) + 3,500 years (written word) = 6,000 years of studying, with the motive of manipulation. Counterfeits like none other. A deceptive mechanism which led ⅓ of the angels to stand on his side of government.

One would instantly think, "Well, as much as Satan's deception is rampant within this world, as long as I have the word of God, I am protected." As we shall see, Satan's most beguiling, deceptive, cunning, bewitching snare is: the word of God. The same tool in which we, the children of God, are to cherish for soul deliverance is the same tool, **when misused**, keeps us in religious bondage.

At the Garden of Eden, Satan added a word, "you shall <u>NOT</u> surely die." In the wilderness with Christ, Satan omitted a word.

I wonder, would I have noticed that omission of Psalm 91?

When Satan quoted the promise, "He shall give His angels charge over Thee," **he omitted the words, "to keep Thee in all Thy ways**;*" that is, in all the ways of God's choosing. Jesus refused to go outside the path of obedience. While manifesting perfect trust in His Father, He would not place Himself, unbidden, in a position that would necessitate the interposition of His Father to save Him from death. He would not force Providence to come to His rescue, and thus fail of giving man an example of trust and submission* (DA 125.2).

Today the enemy quotes the word of God "word for word." This he can do once he misapply the words. And we, being babes of the scriptures, due to negligence or rejection, are swept away with every wind of doctrine. We therefore become drunk with the wine (false doctrine) of Babylon.

CHAPTER 3: WHAT WAS FINISHED?

The question is asked, "Why did Jesus come to this earth?" Majority of us quickly respond, "To die for our sins." So the following question will be, what was finished before he died?

Jesus made statements like: "It is finish...I've done the work of my Father." Statements in which we expect, but statements which will follow his resurrection, if "dying for us" was his only purpose. But that was not the case! According to the gospel of John, **before** Christ yielded up his life he pronounced these words:

And this is life eternal, that they might know thee the only true God, and Jesus Christ, whom thou hast sent. I have glorified thee on the earth: I have finished the work which thou gavest me to do (John 17:3-4).

Notice the context:

Glorifying God was the work Christ came to do. So the plan of redemption has a manifold application. Glorifying God and being made sin for us (being our substitute and surety) go hand in hand. All of our lives, have we been missing the "complete" mission of Christ within the plan of redemption?

On Christ's mission to "destroy the works of the devil," different aspects of this mission by Christ must be considered. Lies were proposed in heaven, even before the creation of this earth, which couldn't be settled by declaration. These lies had to be cleared up by demonstration. Lies of all sort: **1)** laws are not needed [PP 37.2] **2)** He (God) is keeping "us" (creatures) down [PP chapter 1/ reintroduced in Genesis 3:5] **3)** "Ye shall **not** surely die" [Genesis 3:4].

Lie #1: Laws are not needed

Leaving his place in the immediate presence of the Father, Lucifer went forth to diffuse the spirit of discontent among the angels. He worked with mysterious secrecy, and for a time concealed his real purpose under an appearance of reverence for God. **He began to insinuate doubts concerning the laws that governed heavenly beings**, *intimating that though laws might be necessary for the inhabitants of the worlds, angels, being more exalted, needed no such restraint, for their own wisdom was a sufficient guide* (PP 37.2).

Lie #2: God is keeping His creatures "down" (restricted from reaching higher potentials)

And the serpent said unto the woman, Ye shall not surely die: For God doth know that in the day ye eat thereof, then your eyes shall be opened, and ye shall be as gods, knowing good and evil (Gen. 3:4, 5).

Lie #3: Ye shall NOT surely die

*And the serpent said unto the woman, Ye shall **not** surely die (*Gen. 3:4).

There are many other charges against the government of God, but the LIE here which will be emphasized is "Ye shall **not** surely die."

This deception by the devil was the evolution of the false doctrine that the soul is immortal. A doctrine which is still popular in the Christian Church, even 6,000 years (approximately) after its origin.

Ye shall not surely die - was the first sermon ever preached upon the immortality of the soul. Yet this declaration, resting solely upon the authority of Satan, is echoed from the pulpits of Christendom and is received by the majority of mankind as readily as it was received by our first parents (GC 533.2).

How terrible has this been to innocent believers? And how terrible would it be for sincere believers right before the final conflict (Armageddon), where fallen angels will impersonate deceased family members telling them all sorts of lies (DD 41.4, Rev.13:14). There is nothing new under the sun! Satan uses the same moves, just on new fools. Remember the account in 1ˢᵗ Samuel when King Saul acquired for the woman of Endor? Read 1ˢᵗ Samuel 28: 6-19 in correlation to 1SP 376, 377.

There is another message in this subtle lie from Satan in the Garden of Eden, which most of us overlook.

Principle: ==With every effect there is a cause, or, before reaping there must be something sowed.== [Galatians 6:7]

"Ye shall surely die" is the **effect** from disobedience, which was eating of the tree of knowledge of good and evil. This "surely die" was in reference to an eternal separation from God. Although this annihilation became NOT our reality because of Christ, we still see the minute effects of that separation. After our parents excluded themselves from the Garden of Eden through transgression, they witness the reaping of that one act. "They witnessed in drooping flower and falling leaf the first signs of decay. Adam and his companion mourned more deeply than men now mourn over their dead" *(PP 62.1).*

But the question is, what was "really" the **cause**?

By saying, "Hath God said, Ye shall not eat of every tree of the garden? ... Ye shall **not** surely die," Satan was either saying, ==" Eve would not die"== or ==" if she does die it is **not** because of the apparent cause== of unbelief / separation / disobedience." So if death was to come, which even Adam and Eve first recognized through the changes in the atmosphere... the question is: FROM WHO? WHAT WAS IT (DEATH) COMING FROM?

Here is where Satan insinuated that God is a "liar and a murderer."

Drew on Robes of Ignorance – *Had Adam and Eve never disobeyed their Creator, had they remained in the path of perfect rectitude, they could have known and understood God. But when they listened to the voice of the tempter, and sinned against God, the light of the garments of heavenly innocence departed from them; and in parting with the garments of innocence, they drew about them the dark robes of ignorance of God. The clear and perfect light that had hitherto surrounded them had lightened everything they approached; but deprived of that heavenly light, the posterity of Adam could no longer trace the character of God in His created works* (RH March 17, 1904).

Notice what happened to the minds of our first parents in the Garden of Eden. Yes, we know they forfeited the glory that externally covered them. But here we see that the glory was an expression of what was lost spiritually. Never should we believe that while they were naked externally, that they were covered spiritually. Again, we're told that "they drew about them the dark robes of ignorance of God" ibid.

Corruptible Seed

After this subliminal message was implanted in the mind of Eve, it then was accepted into the mind of Adam. As stated previously, the full reality of "You shall surely die" did not happen at the exact time of transgression because of the Son of God, stepping in to take man's place; fulfilling an everlasting promise with the Father that if man were to transgress, He (Christ) will be man's substitute and surety (DA 834.2).

Points to consider:

1. Adam and Eve recognized their "nakedness" after forfeiting the covering of God's righteousness.
2. Sin brings guilt, so Adam and Eve knew that they were wrong. Sin also is "self-justifying," so they started blaming everyone else (Adam → Eve →Serpent).
3. That corruptible seed (the lie of Satan) also brought a tremendous fear of God, causing them to hide. But why? According to God's message, sin = death. So for Adam and Eve, after sinning, to <u>not</u> reap instant death, the thought must have been, "yes we have sinned but we're still alive. So if death comes after sin, it must be, not from the natural result of transgression, but from God." So they were afraid! [Gen 3:10]

This deception was formulated into such a high peak that

Godly men of old became plagued with this perception; ==that God kills those who don't obey his precepts.==

Q: Why do we think the Old Covenant (righteousness by works) mindset of the Jews created so many rigorous laws?

A: Fear!

Q: What was my purpose of serving God, before this truth of His character was understood?

A: Fear!

Q: What did the papacy see? During their massive crusades, where it is recorded that over 50 million Christians were killed by the Papal Church.

A: A God that punish those who don't obey His precepts. (This is the reason why the Papal power punished those who disagreed with their dogmas).

Psychologists agree that perception precedes behavior. Inevitably, a marred picture of God produces a marred experience with Him and one's fellow man.

Note: please don't speed read through this next quotation. Every line is critical.

It was by falsifying the character of God and exciting distrust of Him that Satan tempted Eve to transgress. By sin the minds of our first parents were darkened, their natures were degraded, and their conceptions of God were molded by their own narrowness and selfishness. And as men became bolder in sin, the knowledge and the love of God faded from their minds and hearts. "Because that, when they knew God, they glorified Him not as God," they "became vain in their imaginations, and their foolish heart was darkened." At time Satan's contest for the control of the human family appeared to be crowned with success. During the ages preceding the first advent of Christ the world seemed almost wholly under the sway of the prince of darkness, and he ruled with a terrible power as though through the sin of our first parents the kingdoms of the world had become his by right. **Even the covenant people, whom God had chosen to preserve in the world the knowledge of Himself, had so far departed from Him that they had lost all true conception of His character** (5T 738.3).

Q: Even the covenant people? Whom God had chosen to preserve in the world the knowledge of Himself? Whom were these people?

A: The children of Israel (even the Bible writers).

This reality is not seen by most of Christendom. This reality wasn't seen neither by the Jews. All acts (either blessings or destructions) were looked upon as coming directly from God.

The Jews had forged their own fetters; they had filled for

themselves the cup of vengeance. In the utter destruction that befell them as a nation, and in all the woes that followed them in their dispersion, they were but reaping the harvest which their own hands had sown. Says the prophet: "O Israel, thou hast destroyed thyself:" "for thou hast fallen by thine iniquity." Hosea 13:9; 14:1. **Their sufferings are often represented as a punishment visited upon them by the <u>direct</u> decree of God. It is thus that the great deceiver seeks to conceal his own work.** *By stubborn rejection of divine love and mercy, the Jews had caused the protection of God to be withdrawn from them, and Satan was permitted to rule them according to his will* (GC 35).

Notice that the great deceiver seeks to conceal his own work by the representation of punishments visited upon the Jews as a **<u>direct</u>** decree from God. Mercy!

Q: Where do we find that representation? Who is it often represented by?

A: We find that representation in the Bible.

Notice some representations:

- **Jeremiah:** *I will give their wives unto others... I will send serpents... and they shall bite you, saith the LORD* **(8:10,17)**.
- **Ezekiel:** *Thus saith the LORD; Behold, I am against thee, and will draw forth my sword out of his sheath, and will cut off from the righteous and the wicked* **(21:1-3)**.

- **Isaiah:** *I form the light, and create darkness: I make peace, and create evil: I the LORD do all these things* **(45:7)**.

After reading such passages, what is your honest picture of God? The Bible tells us that Satan has deceived the whole world (Rev. 12:9). We all were brought up hearing the good news of God especially that which was proclaimed 2,000 years ago by the Son of God. This produced a love which melts our hearts, causing us to worship Him in spirit and in truth. But what about that deep seated fear that causes one to tremble when passing through those Old Testament accounts? Even some of those in the New, particularly those of Revelation.

Stay with me please, because throughout this book, information discovered will be to some revolutionary; but at the same time liberating. It is the goodness of God that leads one to repentance (Rom 2:4). As we continue throughout this book, we will see "line upon line, precept upon precept", a clearer understanding of the character of God.

Note: *The Jews, through their sacred literature, spoke much of one eternal all-powerful God, and* **very little** *of a distinctly inferior evil adversary who had at one time been created perfect (Eze. 28:14-19), but who later became the author of all sin* (Study Bible with Ellen G. White

Comments p.1094).

Reread this note and then let's analyze the thought.

This is so important to grasp. Here we are told that the Jews rarely spoke of the archenemy of God. This shows also in the Bible, where things which happened, either good or bad, are attributed to the "hands of God."

This was a time where these men's knowledge of God's character wasn't as clear as it is now, being that we see God's character "without a veil" in Jesus Christ. <u>Nevertheless, these men were heart loyal to the God of heaven</u>. This loyalty was an echo from heaven, where even the unfallen angels kept their loyalty to God's government at a time when lingering questions puzzled their minds because of the charges from Lucifer.

Not until the death of Christ was the character of Satan clearly revealed to the angels or to the unfallen worlds. *The archapostate had so clothed himself with deception that even holy beings had not understood his principles. They had not clearly seen the nature of his rebellion (DA 758.3).*

Q: Why did it take unfallen minds (angels and beings from unfallen worlds) over 4,000 years to see the character of Satan?

A: Mysteriously, these unfallen/high intelligent beings

only could comprehend the character of God (in contrast to that of Satan) through the church. **So as long as we (humans) did not see God as He is, the angels could not see God as He is.**

Notice the words of Paul:

*To the intent that now unto the principalities and powers in heavenly places **might be known by the church** the manifold wisdom of God* (Ephesian 3:10).

Notice the words of Peter:

*Unto whom it was revealed, that not unto themselves, but unto us they did minister the things, which are now reported unto you by them that have preached the gospel unto you with the Holy Ghost sent down from heaven, **which things the angels desire to look into*** (1 Pet. 1:12).

These scriptures express the reality of what's called the Circuit of Beneficence. This is an eternal reality of the Godhead which is exemplified in the order of His creation. That which is summarized in 1st Corinthians 12:18-21 is applicable to the church universal (including those in Christ, the unfallen angels, and other unfallen beings from unfallen worlds). In summary, as much as angels are ministering spirits for our sake, we too play a big part in this great controversy of good vs. evil. **We are witnesses of God for their sake**, and of course others as well.

CHAPTER 4: CHRIST; THE KEY TO UNLOCK MYSTERIES

Born in Bethlehem, the child Christ Jesus attracted the whole universe to witness whom God really is. There was not a better time for light to enter the world. During the time of Christ, everything and everyone was backward, including the people entrusted with the oracles of God. In approximately 33 ½ years, the sons of God (angels and unfallen worlds) got a better picture of the God they serve.

*God, who at sundry times and **in divers manners spake** in time past unto the fathers by the prophets, hath in these last days **spoken unto us by his Son**, whom he hath appointed heir of all things, by whom also he made the worlds; Who being the brightness of his glory and the express image of his person, and upholding all things by the word of his power, when he had by himself purged our sins, sat down on the right hand of the Majesty on high (Hebrew 1:1-3).*

J.B Phillips translation: (Hebrew 1:1)

*God, who gave our forefathers many **different glimpses of the truth** in the words of the prophets, has now, at the end of the present age, given us **the truth** in the Son.*

Q: Why were the prophets spoken to in fragments?

A: "How inspiration work" is an education we all need to comprehend. We often rebut in religious conversations by saying "the Bible says so"; in sincerity not knowing what we're actually saying. The Bible says a lot, but the question should be asked, "What does the Bible mean?"

Christ, the express image of the Godhead, is the only example of God's thoughts made audible. Even so; Christ, because of the dullness of our spiritual ears, had to speak to us sometimes in parables.

Note: Before the incarnation, God spoke to humanity **through** Christ. But while on earth, God spoke to humanity **in** Christ.

*Ever since Adam's sin, the human race had been cut off from direct communion with God; the intercourse between heaven and earth had been through Christ; but now that Jesus had come "in the likeness of sinful flesh" (Romans 8:3), the Father Himself spoke. He had before communicated with humanity **through** Christ, now He communicated with humanity **in** Christ (DA 116.2).*

Through Christ

From[Father]

↓ ↓ ↓

Through[Son]

↓ ↓ ↓

By[Spirit]

↓ ↓ ↓

To[Humanity] - plagued with traditional falsehoods.

In Christ

From[Father]

↓ ↓ ↓

Through[Son]

↓ ↓ ↓

By[Spirit]

↓ ↓ ↓

note: being that the "through" agent of the Godhead became the God-Man (Jesus), the "through" also became the "to", or "in" agency.

*In Christ, the message is unfiltered.

To make this clearer, let's examine how inspiration work.

*The Bible is written by inspired men, **but it is not God's mode of thought and expression**. It is that of humanity. God, as a writer, is not represented. Men will often say such an expression is not like God. But God has not put Himself in words, in logic, in rhetoric, on trial in the Bible. **The writers of the Bible were God's penmen, not His pen**. Look at the different writers. <u>**It is not the words of the Bible that are inspired, but the men that were inspired.**</u>*

==Inspiration acts not on the man's words or his expressions but on the man himself, who under the influence of the Holy Ghost is imbued with thoughts. But the words receive the impress of the individual mind.== **==The divine mind is diffused==**==. <u>The divine mind and will is combined with the human mind and will; thus the utterances of the man are the word of God</u>== (1SM 21.1).

The Inspired Mind

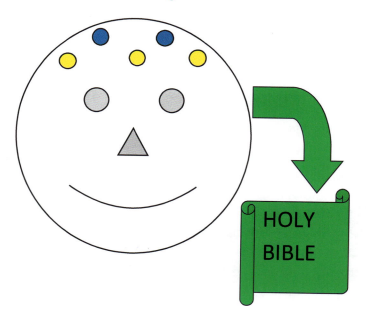

Yellow = Holy Spirit imbues the mind with thoughts

Blue = Preconceived traditional ideas

Green = Divine mind combined with the human mind, giving us the "word of God".

* The colors yellow and blue **combined** gives us the color green.

Notice the parallel line of thought, just in different words:

*Now it is this same Holy Spirit who takes the inner thinking of God and makes it known to his prophets. He does this by "expressing spiritual truths in spiritual words." Thus, it is not a mechanical symbiosis between the divine and the human, but instead a living assimilation between the skills and personally of the writers and the mind of God takes place. Accordingly, all that has gone into the preparation of the writer, the vocabulary, the metaphors of life, the occupation entered prior to the call of God, all play a real part in the "teaching" experience of preparing the speakers for their roles as prophets (*Hard Sayings of the Bible p.69*).*

- As many today wear glasses to complement their blurry vision, so with us, we must approach the "words of God" through the lens of THE "WORD of GOD," Jesus Christ. In Christ, the words of God are ==yellow==, not ==green== (illustration). In Christ, we have scriptural freedom, not bondage. In Christ, we're motivated by love, not fear. Amen!

A Way of Escape

As I examine, through the grace of God, history (both ancient and recent) in the light of: **1)** "kingdoms conquering kingdoms" **2)** steps from bondage to freedom (religiously and secularly) **3)** truly understanding the word of God, etc.

One common denominator stands out: ……. **TIME**

1) "Kingdoms conquering kingdoms" - for example, when Cyrus (the king of ancient Persia) overthrew the empire of Babylon. This wasn't something planned out in a day! We're told that the army of Cyrus spent years plotting this overtake. Seasons of scouting; awaiting the perfect opportunity. (Read more: Great Empires of Prophecy by A.T. Jones)

2) Steps from bondage to freedom - think back on the experience of Harriet Tubman. Think of the stories of many escapes from these modern day, highly secured prisons. Men who were on life sentences, spent 10 to 20 years to map out an escape.

Note: Now these are both "secular" examples. What about in the spiritual realm?

3) Truly understanding the word of God - throughout the history in which we refer to as the "Dark Ages," Satan, through the Papal church, kept the word of God from the children of God. During a time in history, in which the prophet Isaiah prophesied as being a time of "gross darkness," Satan has kept the word of God from the children of God. The time of "gross darkness" is now! Darkness is a result of not having THE light of the world, which is Jesus Christ (Isaiah 60:2).

One may say, "How can it be so dark if we're living in a time where the word of God is available more than any time before?" One may continue to reason that "we're living in an era where Bibles are: in hotels, every home, on cell phones, etc." The question now deepens in this individual's mind, "how can it truly be considered a time of gross darkness?"

The answer to this humble question is simple. Most, God fearing/bible believing/professed Christians **don't** read the word of God; as they ought. Yes, we have Bibles all over our homes and workplace. Yes, we have the word of God with us, via cell phone; at all times. But so did the Jews! Just as complacent we are with merely having the word of God, so they (the Jews) made broad their phylacteries (Matt 23:5).

Here was a people who wore leather straps (headbands) with oracles of God written externally on their foreheads, but rejected the One whom came to write the law of God, internally, on their hearts (Hebrew 8:10 , John 1:10-11).

- How about us?
- Do we spend enough time with the Lord?
- Do we meditate on the life of Christ?
- Are we truly about our Father's business? (Luke 2:41)
- Are we satisfied with sitting at the feet of pastors? Or Jesus?

Let's spend time with the Word of God. Not merely reading or having the words of God, but let us become one with the LIVING WORD of GOD, Jesus Christ... our only hope!

CHAPTER 5: THE GOSPEL CHART

In this chapter we will examine 3 out of the 4 books which gives us primarily the historical accounts of the life, death and resurrection of Jesus Christ. This chart will help us comprehend more that "**the men of the Bible were inspired, not the words**."

Have you ever wondered:

- Why are the sayings of Jesus slightly different in the different accounts of the gospel?

This was something that puzzled me as a youth, because when I read the "red" lettering in the gospel I was told those where the words of Jesus; which in proper explanation is true.

But why was Mark's words not identical to that of Matthew's? I knew that the Bible writers were inspired years after the death of Christ to put these accounts together, but I guess I was missing still one important factor. The factor was "how" these men were inspired to do such a blessed thing.

*While reading this chart remember how inspiration works. Although different words, there is one heartbeat of truth and understanding.

Matthew	Mark	Luke
4:4 It is written, Man shall not live by bread alone, but by every word that proceedeth out of the mouth of God.		**4:4** It is written, That man shall not live by bread alone, but by every word of God.
26:29 But I say unto you, I will not drink henceforth of this fruit of the vine, until that day when I drink it new with you in my Father's kingdom.	**14:25** Verily I say unto you, I will drink no more of the fruit of the vine, until that day that I drink it new in the kingdom of God.	**22:18** For I say unto you, I will not drink of the fruit of the vine, until the kingdom of God shall come.
20:25-28 ye know that the princes of the Gentiles exercise dominion over them, and they that are great exercise authority upon them. But it shall not be so among you: but whosoever will be great among you, let him be your minister. And whosoever will be chief among you, let him be your servant: Even as the Son of man came not to be ministered unto, but to minister, and to give his life a ransom for many.	**10:42-45** Ye know that they which are accounted to rule over the Gentiles exercise lordship over them; and their great ones exercise authority upon them. But so shall it not be among you: but whosoever will be great among you, shall be your minister: And whosoever of you will be the chiefest, shall be servant of all. For even the Son of man came not to be ministered unto, but to minister, and to give his life a ransom for many.	**22:25-27** The kings of the Gentiles exercise lordship over them; and they that exercise authority upon them are called benefactors. But ye shall not be so: but he that is greatest among you, let him be as the younger, and he that is chief, as he that doth serve. For whether is greater, he that sitteth at meat, or he that serveth? Is not he that sitteth at meat? But I am among you as he that serveth.

This chart is only a synopsis of the many examples of Christ's words which gives an illustration on how inspiration works. Remember earlier in chapter 4, the thought was established that the men of the bible were inspired **not** the words. This could be further seen here by the same accounts of Jesus speaking; being that the exact words are not recorded. This is not saying that there is not one heart beat throughout the bible, because it is. ==What this is illustrating is that we must see beyond mere words, and allow the spirit of God to embed in us the meaning.==

Why is this important?

As we shall see, and as we may already comprehend throughout Christianity, is that the "war" is not solely with Christianity and "the world," but shamefully Christianity vs. Christianity. Over 42,000 different sects of professed Christians in this world. All proclaiming to hold the Bible as their guide book, but paradoxically coming to different ends of different roads. This reality is grounded in the fact of us Christians not taking an honest, holistic approach with the Bible.

Q: Why is this so?

A: It is easier to not dig deep. It is easier to take what my pastor says as the final authority. It is easier to simply be at ease!

CHAPTER 6: Psalms 18:25-26

With the merciful thou wilt shew thyself merciful;

With an upright man thou wilt shew thyself upright;

With the pure thou wilt shew thyself pure;

With the froward thou wilt shew thyself froward.

Recap: How inspiration works

THROUGH CHRIST	**IN CHRIST**
Father (from)	Father (from)
⬇	⬇
Son (through) - [DA 116]	Son (through)
⬇	⬇
Spirit (By)	Spirit (by)
⬇ - [1SM 21.2] - [1SM 22.2]	⬇
Servants (to) – [5T 738.2] [5T 738.3]	Servant (to)
⬇	⬇
Writings (combined: Divine mind and the human mind).	Note: the "through" agent became the "to" agent, allowing the thought of God to be manifested unfiltered.
*Combination of yellow/blue = green	*Filter = simply saying, Passing through.

- "Ever since Adam's sin, the human race had been cut off from direct communion with God; the intercourse between heaven and earth had been through Christ, but now that Jesus had come 'in the likeness of sinful flesh" (Rom 8:3), the Father Himself spoke. He had before communicated with humanity **through Christ**; now he communicated with humanity **in Christ**" (DA 116).

- "==It is not the words of the Bible that are inspired, but the men that were inspired==. Inspiration acts not on the man's words or his expressions but on the man himself, who, under the influence of the Holy Ghost, is imbued with thoughts. But the words receive the impress of the individual mind. The divine mind is diffused. <u>The divine mind and will is combined with the human mind and will; thus the utterances of the man are the word of God</u>" (1SM 21.2).

- "Through the inspiration of His Spirit the Lord gave His apostles truth, to be expressed ==according to the development of their minds== by the Holy Spirit. But the mind is not cramped, as if forced into a certain mold (1SM 22.2).

- "It was by falsifying the character of God and exciting distrust of Him that Satan tempted Eve to transgress. By sin the minds of our first parents were darkened…" (5T 738.2)

- "Even the covenant people, who God had chosen to preserve in the world the knowledge of Himself, had so far departed from Him that they had lost all true conception of His character" (5T 738.3).

The Inspired Mind

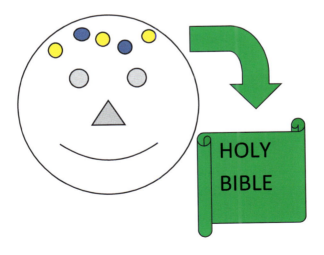

==Yellow== = Holy Spirit imbues the mind with thoughts

Blue = preconceived traditional ideas

Green = Divine mind combined with the human mind, giving us the 'word of God".

Understanding How God Meets Us Where We Are

With the merciful thou wilt shew thyself merciful; with an upright man thou wilt shew thyself upright; with the pure thou wilt shew thyself pure; and with the froward (perverse) thou wilt shew thyself froward (Psalms 18:25-26).

In this chapter we will examine a deeper understanding on the character of God. The ancient prophet Isaiah said that there is a "gross darkness" that covers the people, and Ellen G. White states that this darkness is a misapprehension of who God is (Isaiah 60:1-3; DA 22).

As messengers of the last message of mercy, which is a revelation of God's character, we are up against the world and the church (at large). As darkness deepens in this earth so shall our light grow deeper in the understanding of our Creator. The Lord reveals His glory (His character) continually and it is our duty to "follow on" to understand our wonderful God, not being stagnant at a "need of milk" comprehensive level (Hosea 6:3; Hebrew 5:11-14).

Examples of Growth:

MILK	STRONG MEAT
God doesn't destroy *Read God's Character by Elliot Douglin (appendix 3 gives you a sneak peek)	God **CAN'T** destroy (destruction is contrary to His infinite nature of life).
God withdrew	God is "pushed back" by human choices. He withdraws only when it's not righteously possible for Him to remain in His role as protector, or sustainer. Of course this is different from "removing the hedge" from His righteous witnesses, like Job.
Oh!!!... that's just Bible Language	Explaining **why** the "language" is so. Elaborating on how inspiration works. Usually this removes the patriarch, prophet or apostle out of the mind of the people, as an "idol". We need to be reminded that "even the covenant people" had a dim perception of the character of God. And this don't contradict their upright experience in the Lord.

A Holistic Approach

Similar to the gospel, there are many "character of God" understandings floating around. This is not to condemn anyone's understanding, but this is to recognize that Satan is at work to "half-truth" the believers of God. This simply means that he will flatter our thinking with just enough truth to satisfy our spiritual discernment, but intrigue just enough error to cause us to have slight doubts about God.

Examples of the enemy's work: Using the truth to defend a lie

Using a truth	to	Defend a lie

Using a truth	Defend a lie
"and fire came down from God out of heaven, and devoured them." Rev 20:9	Being that "the LORD is righteous in all his ways and holy in all his works" (Psalms 145:17), Satan developed the false doctrine of "righteous killing."
Romans 1: For the wrath of God = God gave them up.	If God directly killed them or "gave them up," the end result is still the same (which is death). Being that God is the source of life, He is "somewhat" responsible for death.
Jesus is the "express image" of God. Heb. 1:3	Even Jesus in the temple showed a "righteous indignation" by making a scourge and driving people out and overthrowing the tables. (elaboration needed)

On the other hand, the true understanding of God's wrath is abroad in many lands. Truly "7,000 knees have not bowed" to the false doctrine of who God is. Individuals are seeing Romans 1 in light of God respecting men's choice. People are comprehending the reality of sowing and reaping (Galatians 6; James 1). Through diligent study, some are recognizing that those who hate God loves death (Proverbs 8). Although, like every other doctrine, there is always room for growth in understanding, of course without straying away from the foundational truth. For example, there are many who see clearly the mechanism of the Flood and Sodom and Gomorrah. Some even comprehend how inspiration work, including the truth of the ancient cultural belief of attributing everything to God ("God did this and God did that").
*Read Appendix 3 (for insight on Sodom/Flood).

- What about when the prophets heard the Lord say something audibly?
- It was not there mind that was impress upon, but they literally heard the voice of God. So how do we reconcile the apparent dark characteristics in the words of God, which was heard directly by the prophets?
- If God "can't" destroy, why does He say that He will? Not in relation to inspiration, but directly in relation to God speaking. Not through the prophets via "being moved upon," but speaking to the prophets in: person, dream or vision.

Here is where our journey begins. But before we head down the promise land of "reasoning together," let's gas up our vehicle with some fundamental understandings.

Fundamental Understandings

- God is righteous in ALL His ways and holy in all His works (Psalm _____)
- God is light and in Him is no darkness AT ALL (1st John _____)
- God character is eternal; changeless (James _____, Malachi _____, Hebrew _____)
- God never ordained polygamy (Genesis _____)
- God didn't want Israel to see war, let alone fight with the sword (Exodus _____)
- God didn't establish Israel to have a king (1st Samuel _____)
- God was not a "fan" of stoning (John _____)

*fill in the blank please = (___)

This is in no way all the things in the Bible that "seem" as if God was for, in which He really wasn't.

Why so often do we see God commanding war? Or instructing the patriarchs to treat all **wives** equal? Why did He choose a king? Why was there commanding of stoning, from the Lord? These are questions we ask ourselves. These are the questions which after so long of going unanswered causes many to sway away from the faith of God.

Choice

Free choice is talked about much, but understood little. In everything that seems "to the left" when reading the Bible, one must know that it is ultimately a result of human choice of perversion. **If we're stopped from choosing the wrong route, especially after God has given us ample evidence of the right route, ultimately we never had free choice.** But when we see God adapting to that choice, it means that He is truly respecting it, and at the same time influencing us through His love to choose not that way of destruction but His way of life. This is the understanding "God meeting us where we are."

Face to Face (not inspired through the conscience)

Majority of what we call the word of God is manifested through inspiration, where the Spirit of God moved upon the minds of the servants, mingling the will of God with that of man (1SM 1). As this was explained in the earlier chapters of this book, let us now examine when God spoke to the prophets directly or audibly.

- How do we reconcile that "language"?
- It's not a mingling of pure thoughts from God with perverse understandings of man, right?
- We can't easily say "Bible Language" in this particular aspect of the word of God, because on these occasions the words are literally heard.

Example: Face to Face

(Ex. 33:9-11)

v9 And it came to pass, as Moses entered into the tabernacle, the cloudy pillar descended, and stood at the door of the tabernacle, and the LORD talked with Moses. **v10** And all the people saw the cloudy pillar stand at the tabernacle door: and all the people rose up and worshipped, every man in his tent door. **v11** And the LORD spake unto Moses face to face, as a man speaketh unto his friend.

"God said" and "Thus saith the Lord" is mentioned in the Bible hundreds of times. Many times the prophets use this expression to inform their listeners (or readers) on the authority of what they (the prophets) are saying. We, even in our day, use the same expression once the Lord placed something on our hearts. We typically say "God told me" or "the Spirit said"; not meaning that we literally heard Him audibly say it. But Moses is one of the few who spoke (literally) with God. So let us grab some examples of God speaking with him directly, and examine the "seemingly" harshness of God.

In Moses' last speech (Deut. 32: 1-52), the Israelites were given historical accounts of the wonderful dealings of God with His people. Again, these accounts are different from a prophet being inspired through the mind. Henceforth, we could first take it literally, **AS IT IS**, and then we would

==explain **WHY IT IS**.==

Moses repeating what God said

v23 I will heap mischiefs upon them; I will spend mine arrows upon them.

v24 They shall be burnt with hunger, and devoured with burning heat, and with bitter destruction: I will also send the teeth of beasts upon them, with the poison of serpents of the dust.

v39 See now that I, even I, am he, and there is no god with me; **I kill, and I make alive; I wound, and I heal: neither is there any that can deliver out of my hand.**

v42 I will make mine arrows drunk with blood, and my sword shall devour flesh; and that with the blood of the slain and of the captives, from the beginning of revenges upon the enemy.

<mark style="background-color: lightgreen">What do we say to this? Bible Language? Not quite, more like God's language!!!</mark>

But notice our scriptural reading,

With the merciful thou wilt shew thyself merciful; with an upright man thou wilt shew thyself upright; with the pure thou wilt shew thyself pure; and **with the froward thou wilt shew thyself froward** (Psalm 18:25-26).

Q: Which of these, of Psalm 18, was God dealing with?

A: a froward, stiff-necked people

Q: So how did God meet them?

A: In a froward, stiff-necked approach

God says, treat your **wives** equal Exodus 21:10	because, they chose to be polygamist PP 145.1	Originally, God ordained every man a **wife** Genesis 2:24
God says, go kill this nation (and that nation)	because the Israelite chose the swords which came to shore after the Egyptians died in the red sea (Ex 14:30; Heb. 11:1; John 21:25) *read appendix 2	Before this theocratic government God simply gave the rejecters of His love over to themselves, which ended in natural (uncontrolled) calamities
God gave us the commandments in a "thou shall not" linguistic	because coming out of Egypt we were so use to a "Thou shalt and shall not" type of commanding	Before, the laws were orally transmitted to the generations, kept in the hearts of men
God accepted our old covenant promises	because we had an old covenant mindset coming out of Egypt	Before it was a new covenant reality of receiving life to live
God chose a king	because we wanted a king like the other nations	Before He was our King of kings

God said He will do this and do that	because the people thought whatever happen is because of God's doing	This doctrine of God being an executor of those who rejects Him was accepted in Eden *chapter 3

All of these examples are an illustration of God meeting us where we are. ==One should definitely notice that God "meeting us where we are" does not mean that He wants us to stay there. He wants us to grow up in our understanding and experience His way, which is THE WAY (Acts 17:30).==

We can't learn enough about the principle of FREE CHOICE!

- If God originally ordained one man for one wife and you choose to marry multiple (polygamy), and He stops you, did you really have free choice?
- If God shows you how He "defeats" nations (Egypt) and you choose to pick up their same sword; if He stops you, did you really have free choice?
- If God shows you how He rule as King, and you want another king; if He stops you from getting a king, did you really have free choice?

God is so sweet that He doesn't just give us free choice, but He gives ample reason for one to exercise their free will by choosing His way. Now if we reject His way, He sadly respect it, meets us where we are, and do His all to win us back to His perfect way.

Traditional Beliefs

One of the hardest thing to unlearn is a traditional belief. One thing about God is that He, in His love, will often meet that false understanding of an individual or nation (at whatever level they are at), and still influence a transformation of experience. Although we "pride" on intellectual understandings, which we ought to stride for (not pride on), God many times left the intellectual misunderstanding at whatever stage of ignorance one was. While, at the same time using that "intellectual misunderstanding" as a "mean" to get to an "end," which was to influence a reformation of experience of one's character; which is the fitting up for the restoration of the new Eden (heaven).

What am I saying with all of this?

Notice Job: A man who was considered perfect from heaven, but who had an incomplete intellectual understanding of the characteristics and workings of God.

Job 1: Perfect man

Job 38: Ignorant man

Q: Why didn't God in His infinite wisdom explain the mechanism of His wrath, when the people thought otherwise?

Q: Why didn't He remind them of the new covenant experience, when they went into their own ways?

A: Intellectual darkness takes time to give way to light. Experiential darkness is a quicker way to reformation versus the intellectual darkness.

What does this mean?

<u>We have examples of Christ dealing with men **in** their ignorance (of truth), but yet drawing them (while still in their ignorance) to a reformation guide of behavior.</u>

In this next chapter we will see the "express image" of God, Christ himself, truly define the character of God, which will unlock all mysteries concerning God's "seemingly" harsh words in the Bible. Here we will see how there was a false belief, and with that same false belief, Christ spoke in that "false concept" to bring out (illustrate) a deeper and true concept of life.

So keep in mind the thought, that when speaking with a people who was froward or perverse; what type of God we serve. A God that will meet us in our perverseness of understanding to draw us, in our very false understanding, to a conclusive repentant experience.

Bear with me in this thought, because as we continue, we will see that God in his wisdom never violates a principle of righteousness to meet us in our ignorance. Never! (This will be explained in the chapter: Structural vs. Functional.)

CHAPTER 7: The Rich Man and Lazarus (Luke 16:19-31)

v19 *There was a certain rich man, which was clothed in purple and fine linen, and fared sumptuously every day:* **v20** *And there was a certain beggar named Lazarus, which was laid at his gate, full of sores,* **v21** *And desiring to be fed with the crumbs which fell from the rich man's table: moreover the dogs came and licked his sores.* **v22** *And it came to pass, that the beggar died, and was carried by the angels into Abraham's bosom: the rich man also died, and was buried;* **v23** *And in hell he lift up his eyes, being in torments, and seeth Abraham afar off, and Lazarus in his bosom.* **v24** *And he cried and said, Father Abraham, have mercy on me, and send Lazarus, that he may dip the tip of his finger in water, and cool my tongue; for I am tormented in this flame.* **v25** *But Abraham said, Son, remember that thou in thy lifetime receivedst thy good things, and likewise Lazarus evil things: but now he is comforted, and thou art tormented.* **v26** *And beside all this, between us and you there is a great gulf fixed: so that they which would pass from hence to you cannot; neither can they pass to us, that would come from thence.* **v27** *Then he said, I pray thee therefore, father, that thou wouldest send him to my father's thence.* **v28** *For I have five brethren; that he may testify unto them, lest they also come into this place of torment.* **v29** *Abraham saith unto him, they have Moses and the prophets; let them hear* them. **v30** *And he said, Nay, father Abraham: but if one went unto them from the dead, they will repent.* **v31** *And he said unto him, if they hear not Moses and the prophets, neither will they be persuaded, though one rose from thee dead.*

<u>Key Lessons taught in this parable</u>

A. It is in this life that men determine their destiny.
B. There is no probationary period after death.
C. By his own choice man fixes a gulf between him and God.
D. The parable draws a contrast between the wealthy who do not make God their trust and poor who have trusted God.

Q: Why did Christ have the rich man alive in hell (hades or the grave)?

A:

1. Christ met the people on their own ground.
2. The doctrine of a conscious state of existence between death and the resurrection was held by many at that time. **Jesus drew the idea for the story from a common Jewish belief- contrary to Scriptures to be sure, but nonetheless a current Jewish belief.** (This is attested by the Jewish historian Flavius Josephus in his "Discourse to Greeks Concerning Hades.")

3. He framed His parable so as to teach important truths through their preconceived opinions.

"In this parable Christ was meeting the people on their own ground. The doctrine of a conscious state of existence between death and the resurrection was held by many of those who were listening to Christ's words. **The Saviour knew of their ideas, and He framed His parable so as to inculcate important truths through these preconceived opinions** .He held up before His hearers a mirror wherein they might see themselves in their true relation to God. **He used the prevailing opinion to convey the idea He wished to make prominent to all**- that no man is valued for his possessions; for all he has belongs to him only as lent by the Lord" (COL 263).

This here is a very deep concept of God that we in Christendom overlook. Christ uses a perverted belief to bring out a deep truth. Christ uses a perverted belief to draw the people to a reformation in their practical experience. This says a lot about God. While the truth indeed sets us free, **I see God numerous times meeting us in our intellectual darkness while at the same time drawing us to an experiential restoration.**

Why is this so?

To my thinking, as we examine the plan of restoration (or the plan of redemption), our "fitting" up for the glorious kingdom, or our sanctification, is grounded on our experience (character). Notice these words carefully please, OUR "FITTING" UP FOR THE GLORIOUS KINGDOM, OR OUR SANCTIFICATION, IS GROUNDED ON OUR EXPERIENCE (CHARACTER). This is not to neglect our intellect, because our knowledge of God, His workings, and His oracles deepens our experience.

As stated earlier, Job was pronounced from heaven perfect and upright in Job 1. In Job 38, the Lord explained to him how he was not clear of His (God) workings. **This attest that Job's "perfection" was based on his experience (relationship) with the Lord, not his intellectual understanding of the Lord.** Also, in the book of Romans Paul explains how there are people who might not have the instructions or oracles of God, but are a "law unto themselves." Meaning, that the admonition we get through the word of God (intellectually), one may receive through the calling of their hearts (experientially).

"For not the hearers of the law are just before God, but the doers of the law shall be justified. For when the Gentiles, which have not the law, do by nature the things contained in the law, these, having not the law, are a law unto themselves: which **shew** the work of the law written in their hearts, their conscience also bearing witness, and their thoughts the mean while accusing or else excusing one another" (Romans 2: 13-15).

I read something a few months ago that confirmed this thought of God meeting us where we are (in intellectual darkness) to establish an experiential ripening.

"The classic illustration of God's incredible willingness to descend to our human level is a story about Ellen White and Joseph Bates. Evidently, when Bates first met Mrs. White, he wasn't quite convinced of her prophetic gift. Then one afternoon she went into vision while he was in the room, and in vision she saw planets with moons---first she saw one with four, which Bates recognized as Jupiter; then one with seven (Saturn), and one with six (Uranus). Bates knew astronomy, and he knew that Ellen White did not. So he was convinced of her prophetic gift.

"How many moons do we see circling these planets today? Jupiter has sixty-two; Saturn, thirty-one; and Uranus, twenty-seven! But if God had shown these numbers to Mrs. White back in her day, Bates would have disavowed her gift. **God showed her exactly the number that corresponded to the knowledge available at that time.**

"This model says the whole Bible and all Mrs. White's books are absolutely inspired. ==It also suggests what we should do when we read passages that just don't seem to fit the highest and clearest pictures of God that we've==

==found in Christ. It says that rather than rejecting Scripture or attributing terrible characteristics to God, we should simply applaud His grace in "lowering" Himself to speak in terms people of that time and place could understand.==

"This solution preserves the authority, inspiration, and integrity of Scripture while also preserving our non-negotiable anchor points regarding God's character. It allows us to take every passage seriously, searching for why God chose to act or speak in that manner in that situation, and to explore ways of reconciling that with the overall picture of God's character that we find in Scripture. It also allows us to integrate the two seemingly conflicting sets of data about God, understanding one set in terms of the other but respecting it all." (Smith, Dan: *Lord, I Have Questions*)

CHAPTER 8: Structural versus Functional

Christ came in the structure of a sinner (Romans 8:3)	**Christ never functioned as a sinner (1st Peter 2:22)**
God structurally said that He will send His armies to destroy the city of Jerusalem. (Matthew 22:1-14)	**Functionally, after the Jews rejected God with their practices, pushing His protective hedge away, the Roman army in A.D. 70 destroyed the city and the people therein. (GC 35,36)**
God structurally said He will slay, and kill, etc.	**God functionally was rejected (fully) and respected their choosing (sadly), having to give them up (ex: Acts 5 Ananias and Sapphira).**
God structurally answer the prayer of Elijah (1st King 18:37-38)	**Functionally, God was not a part of that fire (1st King 19:11-12; Luke 9:51-56; Matthew 27:46)**

So what happen in 1st King 18?

Elijah prayed for fire to come down. What happen? Fire came down! But in 1st King 19, God said He is not in the midst of destructive fire (1st King 19:12). Also, in Luke 9 when the disciples told Jesus to call down fire to smite the Samaritans, Jesus rebuked them.

And it came to pass, when the time was come that he should be received up, he steadfastly set his face to go to Jerusalem, and sent messengers before his face: and they went, and entered into a village of the Samaritans, to make ready for him. And they did not receive him, because his face was as though he would go to Jerusalem. And when his disciples James and John saw this, they said, Lord, wilt thou that we command fire to come down from heaven, and consume them, even as Elias (Elijah) did? But he turned, and rebuked them, and said, Ye know not what manner of spirit ye are of. For the Son of man is not come to destroy men's lives, but to save them. And they went to another village (Luke 9:51-56).

The mechanism of this situation in 1st King 18 is important to understand. According to Colossians 1:17, all things in Christ consist. And according to 2 Peter 3:7, the heavens and the earth are kept in store by the word of God. Hebrews 1: 3 states that "all things are upheld by the word of his power."

Not in a false doctrinal "pantheistic view", but in the truth as it is; since the fall, all of the subjective laws of nature have been perverted. Our first representative man, Adam, who had dominion over this earth separated himself from God in the Garden of Eden. Therefore in like manner, inevitably caused a separation of every order in nature in which God created and proclaimed to be "very good" (Gen. 1:31). Again, by his word all things consist and are kept in store, both directly (of God's authoritative word) and indirectly (through his ministering angels - Rev 7:1). The "holding together" of this groaning earth and its invisible elements (i.e. wind) is sometimes let lose due to the rejecters of God's mercy. An example of this on a large scale will be at the Universal Flood in the days of Noah, where the Antediluvians fully rejected the protection of the Lord, in which He (God) had to sadly let go of those perverted elements in which were being held in check by His word. Notice the record in **Job 21**. Eliphaz, a "friend" of Job (although coming to Job with a wrong tenor), made some true statements. Here is one of them:

*Hast thou marked the old way which wicked men have trodden? Which were cut down out of time, whose foundation was overflown with a flood: which said unto God, **depart from us**: and what can the Almighty do for them? (v15-17)*

I know the thought came to you, "but the Bible said, that the LORD will destroy man whom He have created from the face of the earth; both man, and beast, and the creeping thing, and the fowls of the air; for it repenteth me that I have made them" (Gen 6:7).

Remember:

"Scriptural language frequently attributes directly to God what he merely permits" (Hard Sayings of the Bible p.197).

On a smaller scale, an example will be at the plains of Sodom and Gomorrah. Like stated earlier, God through His mercy is "holding in check" by His word, things both directly and indirectly. In the case of Sodom & Gomorrah plus more exegesis on the Flood; refer to Appendix 3.

Practical Application for Scriptural Freedom

<u>3 "tions" to shun (while studying the bible)</u>

1. MisinterpretaTION
2. MisapplicaTION
3. Out of contextual-relaTION

Misinterpretation

Be assured:

"Knowing this first, that no prophecy of the scripture is of any private interpretation. For the prophecy came not in old time by the will of man: but holy men of God spake as they were moved by the Holy Ghost" (2 Peter 1:20-21).

Be aware:

Watch out for what I like to call "single brick homes." Meaning, doctrines which are built on **ONE** text, which frequently is out of context.

For example, when a preacher quotes a text, closes his bible, and speaks to the congregation for an hour without qualifying his thoughts with other texts. This is called "single brick homes." These all are doomed to fall.

Misapplication

Be assured:

Old Testament stories in a "literal/local" sense, has an end time "spiritual/worldwide" application.

For example, on the next page you will see a chart of Old Testament "literal realities" applied "spiritually" in the New Testament.

The first Adam – father of a sinful, mortal race	Jesus – the "last Adam"; the father of a sinless, immortal race (1st Cor. 15:45-49)
Eve – Adam's wife	The church – the bride of "the last Adam" (Eph. 5:31,32; Gen 2:23,24)
Melchisedec, the king/priest of Salem	Typified Jesus, "The King of Righteousness," the "King of Peace," who reigns in "the Heavenly Jerusalem" (Heb. 7:2-6; 12:22)
Abraham, the father of the tribes of Israel	"The father of them that believe" (Rom. 4:11-18; 9:7,8; Gal. 3:7-9, etc.)
Isaac, the promised seed	Type of Jesus; also type of those who are Christ's (Matt. 1;1; Gal.3:16; 4:28)
Isaac, miraculously born of a freewoman, was free	Type of Christians who are born again of the Holy Spirit. (Gal.4:28)
Israelites	Christians. (Rom 2:28, 29; 9:7, 8; Gal. 3:29; Rev. 7:4-8; 21:12-14, etc.)

Be aware:

Many are studying prophecies of the Old Testament and applying "Israel" to literal Israel, "Egypt" to literal Egypt, etc. This is a misapplication!

Out of contextual relation

Be assured:

When the writers of the bible wrote, their writings were not separated into chapters. This is important because sometimes starting at the beginning of a chapter to get the context isn't enough. We might have to start from the beginning of the book itself.

Be aware:

When we as the hearers of a message don't take heed from the Bereans of Acts 17:11, where they went back to make sure what Paul was saying was so.

Practical Realities for Scriptural Freedom

1) **Early morning communion** - Mark 1:35
2) **Meditation** - go over what was read in the morning. Recap the spiritual lessons throughout the day.

3) **Health** - exercise/proper nutrition (3rd John 1:2)
4) **Note Taking** - revisiting the pastor's message is important.
5) **Visualize** - the power of the imagination. Pick a book of the bible and visualize the scenes from beginning until...you fall asleep (turn off that television).

JOHN 8:36

If the Son therefore shall make you free, you shall be free indeed.

Chapter 9: Treasures and Vessels

For God, who commanded the light to shine out of darkness, hath shined in our hearts, to give the light of the knowledge of the glory of God in the face of Jesus Christ. But we have this treasure in earthen vessels, that the excellency of the power may be of God, and not of us (2nd Cor. 4:6-7).

This treasure is the light that shine out of darkness. God, who brought forth that light in Genesis 1, also shines in our heart. This light which shines in our hearts is the revelation of the knowledge of the glory (character- Ex.33:18-19) of God in the illustration of Christ.

*Specifically in this context, we as His witnesses are the vessels.

As you read this chart on the next page, note in your mind what the author is saying. Note in your mind what the author is not saying. First off, the author is not saying that there is of no importance in the vessel. The fact that the vessel is the instrument used to house the treasure draws virtue to the vessel; but NOT of itself. The vessel isn't to receive praise. Its duty is to point the viewers to the treasure.

Carefully examine these scriptures and see how they correlate with our theme: Scriptural Bondage.

TREASURE	VESSELS
The Living Word of God (Christ/John 1:1-5)	The BIBLE (John 5:39)
The truth in which the Spirit of God brings to our mind (1st Cor. 1:12; John 16:13)	A pastor that preaches a sermon (Galatians 2:20)
The God of nature (Colossians 1:16)	Nature (Acts 14:15-17; Romans 1:20)
True Understanding (2nd Tim. 2:15; John 14:6)	Words 2nd Peter 3:15-17

Simple indeed! Go over these scriptures, and ponder the overall thought.

Conclusive Thought

I want the reader to be assured that this message is primarily for the author. This book was formulated to share the liberty in which the author is experiencing through this truth. Be reminded that this is a foundation of many other books in which will be released with the theme of "setting the captives free" from scriptural bondage. As the Lord sees fit, different "seemingly" hard sayings of the Bible and different "seemingly" contradictions will be explored in the future. I invite you to read also the appendixes of this book. But before you do that, allow me to agitate your mind in relation to what was learned.

There is a story in the Bible that is written on two different accounts.

1st account = "And again the anger of the LORD was kindled against Israel, and he moved David against them to say, Go, number Israel and Judah" (2nd Sam. 24:1).

2nd account = "And Satan stood up against Israel and provoked David to number Israel' (1 Chron. 21:1).

Here I would want to see if we comprehend this book's theme by exciting our reasoning skills; via these two accounts of the **same** story.

- Why is this so?

- Why are these two accounts attributing two different governments for the "moving upon David?" (1 saying God. The other saying Satan.)

- Is the Bible contradictive?

Note:

According to Jewish tradition the first 24 chapters of 1 Samuel were written by Samuel, and the remainder of 1 Samuel, together with 2 Samuel by **Nathan** and **Gad** (see 1 Chronicles 29:29).

2nd Samuel deals exclusively with the reign of David, from **1011 to 971 B.C**. Please don't miss the thought as we continue. Nathan was a contemporary of David. We know this because of his reproof to David (2nd Sam. 12). Keep this in mind as we point our attention to the historical backdrop of the Chronicles.

The book Ezra and Nehemiah form the historical and literary continuation of the books of Chronicles, and a study of the style and language reveals that they probably had the same author. Jewish tradition (the Talmud) names Ezra as the chief author (Baba Bathra 15a) and Nehemiah as the one who completed the work.

So the setting up of Chronicles was after the return to Judea during the reign of Artaxerxes I (**465-423 B.C.**).

What does all of this signify?

According to Proverbs 4:18, "the path of the just is as the shining light, that shineth more and more unto the perfect day."

==Over 500 years elapsed between the writing of 2nd Samuel and 1st Chronicles. A time in which, if "the light shineth more and more," the people of God will become more liberated from the lies on God. This liberation was heighten by the further revelations of Satan, throughout that time, by Isaiah and Ezekiel.==

So according to the understanding of this book's theme, as the perverted picture of God became clearer (illustrated as the color blue / page 26), so would the words written by men (not God) become lighter green.

Do you get the point?

Think about it. Go over the earlier chapters. Don't rush the thought.

Notice: If God, through His mechanism of "inspiring" prophets is ever the same, how come there are different accounts of the same story?

If the answer is not clear, reread this book. Yes, it is short enough, and it is of high importance that we see God as He truly is. God bless!

APPEDIX 1: Will The Lost Burn Forever?

Rev. 14:11

And the smoke of their torment ascendeth up for ever and ever: and they have no rest day nor night, who worship the beast and his image, and whosoever receiveth the mark of his name.

Rev. 20:10

And the devil that deceived them was cast into the lake of fire and brimstone, where the beast and the false prophet are, and shall be tormented day and night for ever and ever.

Be mindful, this is the same John, whom gave us such beautiful letters on God's character of love. The same John who wrote such profound gospel (the divinity of Christ, the humbling life of Christ, etc.). The same John in which we Christians base our theme text; "for God so love the world that He gave His only begotten son, for who so ever believe in Him shall not"...TORTURE FOREVER? Shall not BURN FOREVER? No, but shall not PARISH!!! But have everlasting life. Which brings to mind Romans 6:23, where "the wages of sin is death." Also, bringing to mind Psalms

37:20 where "the wicked will perish, and shall be consumed away."

Torment Forever? Or Perish?

Is John contradictive? Inspired by God, is this saying that God is contradictive? As we well may know, majority of professed Atheist sincerely don't believe in God because of doctrines which seem to be contradictive. No more misapprehension people! Peter, through inspiration gives us warning that there's no private interpretation of scripture (2 Peter 1:20).

Let us search this matter out.

Jude 7 says that Sodom and Gomorrah are set forth for an example: "*suffering the vengeance of **eternal** fire.*"

The prophet Jonah said he "*went down to the bottoms of the mountains; the earth with her bars was about me **forever**"* (Jonah 2:6).

Exodus 12:24 (speaking of the Passover) says, "*And ye shall observe this thing for an ordinance to thee and to thy sons **forever**.*"

1st Chronicles 23:13 & Exodus 40:15

"*Aaron and his sons were to offer incense **forever**... and to have an **everlasting** priesthood.*"

Summary:

Q: If I was to ask you, after you just got off work, "what did you do today?"

Your answer will probably be, "work, **ALL** day."

==Let's understand, Sodom and Gomorrah is not still burning [2 Peter 2:6]. Their ruins are quite submerged in what we know as the Dead Sea. The prophet Jonah, with his "forever" journey in the great fish's belly was literally 3 days and 3 nights [Jonah 1:17]. That Passover to be observed "forever," ended at the cross [Hebrew 9:24-26]. Aaron, and his sons offer incense "forever?" An "everlasting" priesthood? This priesthood, with its offerings of incense, also ended at the cross [Hebrew 7:11-14].==

Likewise reader, with our modern day linguistics, 8 hours at work is NOT "all day" literally. But, the emphasis is made with intentions of proper understanding of interpretation.

Words & Interpretations

Example of a Greek friend:

Let's say I have a Greek friend, and I give him a call to express how much I appreciate and love him. Although he know enough English to communicate with me, he is grounded more in his Greek language. So when I said **"I love you**," he quickly specified my words by saying, "philia you too." Why did my Greek friend emphasize my English "love" with his Greek "love" (philia)? Because in Greek, there are 4 words for the 1 English word love.

Eros – romantic love (spouse)

Philia – brotherly love (friendship)

Storge – mother and child (kinship)

Agape – unconditional love (God's love for us sinners)

Words & Interpretations

Example of "the car is hot":

If I simply say, "The car is hot." To a mechanic, one needs to check the engine. To a salesman, this is a popular "must have" car. To someone who just got into a leather seated car in the summer time in Miami; the air condition needs to come on. But all I said was that "the car was hot."

God, in His eternal purpose, to extend the family of the Godhead invites all to enter into His rest (Hebrew 4). Most will refuse that invitation and "give themselves up" like Sodom & Gomorrah (Jude 7), or tell God "depart from us" as the Antediluvians (Job 22:17). God, in respect of our choice, has to give one up, to the death one chooses

(Proverbs 8:36). This leaves them where "they shall be as though they had not been (Obadiah 16).

Food for thought

Burning "forever" is not death. It is not the 2nd death (Revelation 20:14).

Even more revelation on the character of God, is how the unrighteous burn. Wishing that no man perish (2nd Peter 3:9), our LORD is pleading with us in these days of probationary time. Not only protecting us from our evil human nature by His spirit, but also protecting us from the winds of strife, which is marked within this sinful world (Revelation 7:1).

That "lake of fire," which will bring Satan and his followers to ashes (Ezekiel 28:18), where "never shalt thou be any more" (v19), is the final "giving up, withdrawal or wrath of God." **Where sin, not God, will destroy the wicked** (James 1:15).

Let's now heed 2nd Peter 3:5-7 in relations to God's mercy to this sinful world. Also, here we will see how our Lord has nothing to do with destruction; even the final destruction.

(v5-7) *For this they willingly are ignorant of, that by the word of God the heavens were of old, and the earth standing out of the water and in the water, whereby the world that then was, being overflowed with water, perished BUT the heavens and the earth, which are now, by the same word are kept in store, reserved unto fire against the day of judgment and perdition of ungodly men.*

*Keep in mind verse 7 (highlighted) of 2nd Peter 3 as you read the next passage.

"As in the flood of water when the foundations of the earth were broken up so that water rushed out from beneath the surface, so the stores of oil and coal still hidden from men in the bowels of the earth will burst forth in flaming torrents upon the surface. The reservoir of fire is held in check, ready to spring forth with spectacular force the next time God withdraw on a global scale. It will manifest at the 2nd coming (Revelation 16:18-21), also at the end of the millennium in heaven (Revelation 20:15)." (Straub, Kevin: As He Is)

2 types of burnings explained

As our previous passage explains, there will be a literal burning, which will be ignited when God sadly gives this "groaning earth" up to the perverted nature it became due to the original separation at the Garden of Eden, as well as the ongoing apostasy of mankind throughout the ages. The elements also in our solar system, known as meteorites (which has sulfur), or biblically spoken as "brimstones" will contribute to that destruction. Predominantly at the great white throne judgment (the 3rd coming of Christ), where sin will be eradicated. But also at Christ's 2nd coming will those "brimstones" fall down.

As gruesome as this may seem to the mind, this is not the most detrimental of the 2 burnings. There is a "burning" of guilt, from total separation of God that will surpass that of physical fire. This is a mental agony that is experienced by those who reject the "remedy" that is given to the world, in Christ. At Calvary an example is given to us, where although Christ, suffering that physical pain of nails, scourging, thirst, etc. It didn't amount to the spiritual/mental agony he felt by being our substitute of reaping what sin cause, which is separation and ultimately death.

Notice this quote:

Upon Christ as our substitute and surety was laid the iniquity of us all. He was counted a transgressor, that He might redeem us from the condemnation of the law. The guilt of every descendant of Adam was pressing upon His heart. The wrath of God against sin, the terrible manifestation of His displeasure because of iniquity, filled the soul of His Son with consternation.

The withdrawal of the divine countenance from the Saviour in this hour of supreme aguish pierced His heart with a sorrow that can never be fully understood by man. ***So great was this agony that His physical pain was hardly felt*** (DA 753).

Burning (soul separation)

As soon as the books of record are opened, and the eye of Jesus looks upon the wicked, they are conscious of every sin which they have ever committed. They see just where their feet diverged from the path of purity and holiness, just how far pride and rebellion have carried them in the violation of the law of God. The seductive temptations which they encouraged by indulgence in sin, the blessings perverted, the messengers of God despised, the warnings rejected, the waves of mercy beaten back by the stubborn, unrepentant heart, all appear as if written in letters of fire. **All behold the enormity of their guilt**. (GC p.666)

National Dictionary of the Psychology states, **"Guilt is in a sense a self-administered punishment."**

"The burning is the agony of loss, hatred, rage, and the realization of the burden of sin, in the soul. It is a burning that only death can relieve. The rod of power is to pass out of God's hands and control as all of that which has been marred by sin will evaporate back into the void from whence it came by His original Word." (Straub, Kevin: As He Is)

So, will the lost burn forever?

Yes, the Bible says so! But what that "forever" mean is crucially important.

Defining "forever"

The expression "for ever and ever" in the Greek means unto ages of ages. This expression is used elsewhere in connection with God or Christ and in these cases expresses endless existence. But the meaning is derived

==from God and Christ with which it is associated. The expression itself does not necessarily mean an endless existence. The punishment of the wicked will be for a certain period but not an unending period which is evident from other scriptures that show the fate of the wicked to be annihilation.==

Examples:

Wicked destroyed

Psalm 145:20; Psalm 101:8; Psalm 37:38; Psalm 92:7; Proverbs 13:13; Proverbs 10:29; Philippians 3:19; 1st Timothy 6:9; 2nd Thessalonian 1:9

They shall perish

Psalm 37:20; Proverbs 19:9; Luke 13:3; 2nd Thessalonian 2:10; 2nd Peter 2:12; Matthew 3:12; Hebrew 6:8; Matthew 13:30; Malachi 4:1, 3

They will be consumed

Isaiah 1:28; Psalm 37:20

Wicked will be devoured

Psalm 21:9; Revelation 20:9; Hebrew 10:27

They should be cut off from the earth

Psalm 37:2, 9, 22, 28, 34, 38; Isaiah 33:12; Proverbs 2:22

The wicked will go into perdition or utter ruin

Hebrews 10:39; 2nd Peter 3:7

How long is forever?

The length of forever is determined by the way it is applied, and the nature of the subject to which it is applied. If we apply it to the area of life and say, God lives forever, or that the saints will live forever, we mean their lives will be endless because God is immortal by nature and the saints will be given immortality. If we say the wicked and Satan will burn forever, we mean as long as they live, which will not be endless because by nature they are mortal and are not given eternal life (1 John 5:12). It does not necessarily mean a condition that never ends. It mean a continuance without a break and the length of continuance depends upon the object to which it is applied. The word tall is like that too. For instance, a tall man may be 6 ½ feet; whereas a tall mountain might be 6,000 feet.

APPENDIX 2: PICKING UP THE EGYPTIAN SWORDS

Exodus 14:30 – *Thus the LORD saved Israel that day out of the hand of the Egyptians; and Israel saw the Egyptians dead upon the sea shore.*

Hebrew 11:1 – *Now faith is the substance of things hoped for, **the evidence of things not seen**.*

John 21:25 – *And there are also many other things which Jesus did, the which, if they should be written every one, I suppose that even the world itself could not contain the books that should be written. Amen.*

*Keep these three scriptures in mind as you follow this thought.

After the Egyptians came to the shore of the Red Sea, do you believe they came to the shore naked? Without armor? Of course not! As they came, so did their weapons come.

How do we know this?

Because soon after, the Israelites had weapons for warfare. It obviously was not God's plan for them to engage in warfare. This is known through the fact that God didn't want them to even "see warfare," let alone engage in it.

Remember choice?

If God would have forced the Israelites not to pick up the Egyptian's weapon, especially after demonstrating to the them how He operates, they ultimately would not have had free moral choice.

==Note:== Reread the scriptures on the previous page. Also, reread the summary and see how things come together. Although, the scriptures does not explicitly confirm how the Israelites got weapons, we can know for sure that God did not rain them from heaven. Christ, as well confirmed that His government "don't' fight." So without contradiction, we know the wars of Israel was not God's way of operation. He, in respect of creature's choice, permitted that "war" reality, monitoring at best the evil in which they chose (i.e. "don't torture, do it quickly" – 1st Sam. 15:3).

==*Be assure that this **PAINS** God.==

APPENDIX 3: ALLOWING THE BIBLE TO INTERPRET ITSELF

(This entire appendix is taken directly from a book entitled God's Character – The Best News in the Universe by Elliot Douglin) *British English – so some words are spelled differently. This is from chapter 15 – Three Outstanding Examples

Here, I would only state 2 examples

God is the Protector. It is His restraining power which holds in check the sin-damaged power of nature, and thereby prevents mankind from passing fully under the malignity of Satan's government of sin.

Though they don't know or don't care, those who don't believe in God have great reason to be thankful for God's mercy and long-suffering in holding in check the cruel, malignant power of Satan's government of sin and the perverted powers of creation on our planet and its solar environs.

Yes, dear reader, God is infinitely merciful, loving, compassionate. He is not willing that any should perish. Destruction is not the result of any change in Him.

"For I am the Lord, I change not; therefore ye sons of Jacob are not consumed." Malachi 3:6

"It is of the Lord's mercies that we are not consumed, because his compassions fail not." Lamentations 3:22

But God is also a God of justice. In mercy He comes near to save and to protect. In justice He leaves the rejectors of His mercy to themselves to reap what they have sown.

"For a small moment have I forsaken thee; but with great mercies will I gather thee. In a little wrath I hid my face from thee for a moment; but with everlasting kindness will I have mercy on thee, saith the Lord thy Redeemer." Isaiah 54:7, 8

"Be not deceived; God is not mocked: for whatsoever a man soweth, that shall he also reap. For he that soweth to his flesh shall of his flesh reap corruption; but he that soweth to the Spirit shall of the Spirit reap life everlasting." Galatians 6:7, 8

==God exercises His justice in the hiding of His face. And remember it is sin that hides God's face from us. Sin separates from God and produces death.==

"But your iniquities have separated between you and your God, and your sins have hid his face from you, that he will not hear." Isaiah 59:2

"Then when lust hath conceived, it bringeth forth sin: and sin, when it is finished, bringeth forth death." James 1:15

When men pass the limits of divine forbearance, that is, when their minds are irreversibly made up that they do not want God, all that God can do is to "hide His face", withdraw His protective restraint and leave the rejectors of His mercy to reap the whirlwinds of destruction from the sown winds of sin. The Spirit of God, persistently resisted, is at last withdrawn from the rejectors of God's mercy and there is left no power to control or to protect from the malignant effects of sin.

'O Lord, the hope of Israel, all that forsake thee shall be ashamed, and they that depart from me shall be written in the earth, because they have forsaken the Lord, the foundation of living waters." Jeremiah 17:13

We shall now turn our attention to three outstanding examples of the exercise of God's justice or wrath and learn more precious lessons about God's wonderful protection on one hand and the malignant nature of sin on the other hand.

ONE: The Flood

"And God saw that the wickedness of man was great in the earth, and that every imagination of the thoughts of his heart was only evil continually. And it repented the Lord that he had made man on the earth, and it grieved him at his heart. And the Lord said, I will destroy man whom I have created from the face of the earth; both man, and beast, and the creeping thing, and the fowls of the air; for it repenteth me that I have made them... And, behold, I, even I, do bring a flood of waters upon the earth, to destroy all flesh, wherein is the breath of life, from under heaven; and every thing that is in the earth shall die." Genesis 6:5-7 and 17

The language is typically punitive, it plainly states that God said, "I will destroy..." "I, even I, do bring a flood of waters..."

By now we should fully understand how such language is to be interpreted. The intensity of sin was so great that it was actually approaching the critical point of separation from God. We are sure of this from Genesis 6:3 and Job 22:15-17.

"And the Lord said, My spirit shall not always strive with man, for that he also is flesh: yet his days shall be an hundred and twenty years." Genesis 6:3

The Spirit of God would continue His work of striving with the antediluvians for only one hundred and twenty years more, (a relatively short time, considering the life-span of humans before the flood).

"Hast thou marked the old way which wicked men have trodden? Which were cut down out of time, whose foundation was overflow with a flood: Which said unto God, Depart from us: and what can the Almighty do for them?" Job 22: 15-17

The antediluvians, in every thought and imagination, told God to leave them alone, to depart from them. And when the minds of men are irreversibly fixed against God and they wish God to depart from them, what can God do? The answer is given in Hosea 4:17.

"Ephraim is joined to idols: let him alone." Hosea 4:17

The antediluvians reached that critical point in sin at which mercy gave way to wrath. They suffered the hiding of God's face, that terrible separation from God caused by sin.

There is a passage in Isaiah where the mechanisms of wrath and mercy are linked to the Flood of Noah.

"For a small moment have I forsaken thee; but with great mercies will I gather thee. In a little wrath I hid my face from thee for a moment; but with everlasting kindness will I have mercy on thee, saith the Lord thy Redeemer. For this is as the waters of Noah unto me: for as I have sworn that waters of Noah should no more go over the earth; so have I sworn that I would not be wroth with thee, nor rebuke thee." Isaiah 54: 7, 8, 9

We have conclusive evidence here that the Antediluvians reached that critical point in rebellion against God when sin separated them irreversibly from God (Isaiah 59:2) but is expressed as: God hiding His face from them, when He forsook them, when He withdrew His Spirit, and when he departed because He was asked to leave. **And, as usual, the Bible describes God as doing what He did not prevent.**

In order to understand how the Flood happened after God withdrew, we must learn about the special geophysical conditions which existed before the Flood.

On the first day of creation-week the earth was submerged in a vast quantity of water.

"In the beginning God created the heaven and the earth. And the earth was without form, and void; and darkness was upon the face of the deep. And the Spirit of God moved upon the face of the waters." Genesis 1:1, 2

One the second day God divided the vast quantity of water into two separate masses: water on the earth and water above the sky or firmament.

"And God said, Let there be a firmament in the midst of the waters, and let it divide the waters from the waters. And God made the firmament, and divided the waters which were under the firmament from the waters which were above the firmament and it was so." Genesis 1:6, 7.

On the fourth day God made two great lights, the Sun and the Moon.

"And God made two great lights; the greater light to rule the day, and the lesser light to rule the night: he made the stars also." Genesis 1:16

The language here in Genesis 1:16 suggests that the Moon, when it was created, was a self-luminous body – a great light, not a mere reflector. This is confirmed by Isaiah who informs us that when all things shall be restored, the Moon will be as bright as our present Sun and the restored Sun will be seven times brighter.

"Moreover, the light of the moon shall be as the light of the sun, and the light of the sun shall be sevenfold, as the light of seven days, in the day that the Lord bindeth up the breach of his people, and healeth the stroke of their wound." Isaiah 30:26

The combined heat of the Sun and Moon supplied more than enough energy to keep the vast quantity of water above the firmament in the vapour state. This vast quantity of water vapour completely surrounded our planet and allowed a mild, beautiful, "air – conditioned" climate all over the earth. They were no frigid north and south poles and no torrid equatorial regions. The beautiful vegetation and the climate was ideal.

In Job 38, God mentioned this cloud or swaddling band of water vapour, that surrounded our planet as a protective garment.

"When I made the cloud the garment thereof, and the thick darkness a swaddlingband for it." Job 38:9

God's infinite power, infinite wisdom and infinite love in His Son through His Spirit maintained that ingenious masterpiece of created geophysical technology in perfect working order.

The antediluvians were blessed with paradise conditions, they were strong, healthy and long-lived, but they rejected God's government of righteousness and as a result wickedness reached unimaginable and unprecedented proportions.

Rain did not fall in the antediluvian world, in fact that was a world so vastly different to our present world that it stretches the mind to grasp it.

All the water on the surface of the planet was in one place and all the dry land mass was in one body – a geographical topography unknown to our present system. During the night as the temperature cooled off, enough condensation occurred to allow a mist or dew to moisten the whole face of the ground. There were no storms, no extremes of climate, no weather disturbances as now exist in our present world. Furthermore, the massive water vapor mantle prevented any beams of sunlight from entering directly into the atmosphere, screening all radiant energy or rays which would have been dangerous to creatures on earth. Man and animals ate fruits and herbs as stated in

Genesis 1:29, indeed everything was conducive to health, vigour and longevity.

The warning given by Noah was ridiculed and rejected. Yet for 120 years God's spirit pleaded with the antediluvians.

Because God foreknew the consequences of sin's irreversible separation, He advised Noah to build an ark, and all who had faith enough to go into that ark would have been saved from the flood.

When Noah and his family were safe in the ark, the angel of God closed the door and for seven days **no change appeared: the antediluvians did not realize that probation was closed, that God had withdrawn and that the Sun and Moon were undergoing drastic changes.** Then 7 days after Noah entered the ark, "all the springs of the great deep burst forth and the floodgates of the heavens were opened. And rain fell on the earth forty days and forty nights." Genesis 7:11, 12 (NIV). Yes, the vast quantity of water above the firmament came down; the Sun had been reduced to its present state, the Moon had gone out. The controlling protective, sustaining power over the elements was no longer present and one great upheaval occurred. **It was the day of judgment for that corrupt civilization. They understood too late that the wages of sin is death. They did not want God and He departed from them.** The Apostle Peter refers to the great change that took place, in 2 Peter 3:3-7.

"Knowing this first, that there shall come in the last days scoffers, walking after their own lusts, And saying, Where is the promise of his coming? For since, the fathers fell asleep, all things continue as they were from the beginning of the creation. For this they willingly are ignorant of, that by the word of God the heavens were of old, and the earth standing out of the water and in the water: Whereby the world that then was, being overflowed with water, perished: But the heavens and the earth, which are now, by the same word are kept in store, reserved unto fire against the day of judgment and perdition of ungodly men." 2 Peter 3:3-7

After the flood the world was so different, so inferior to what it was before! The burial of the immense forests gave rise to the formation of coal and oil, volcanoes and earthquakes. **Thus the next time God withdraws there will be fiery destruction**. 2 Peter 3:7.

The Sun, Moon, the entire Solar System and even beyond were profoundly affected by the terrible separation from God, which caused the Flood of Noah's day. Astronomical pictures of the moon and planets of the present Solar System show chaotic surfaces with volcanic activity and fierce wind storms in other words, the forces of nature on the planets are as disordered as they are here on earth. We know that God made a perfect creation in the beginning so wherever we see disorder we know it is the result of the sin problem on earth.

There can never again be a global flood as in Noah's day because the vast quantity of water vapour, which was above the firmament, came down at the Flood. Direct beams of light have since then been entering our atmosphere and whenever such direct beams pass through an area of cloudiness there is refraction of the light producing the spectrum of colours found in white light. This is called the rainbow. Whenever we see it we should remember the changes in geography which occurred at the Flood.

"And I will established my covenant with you; neither shall all flesh be cut off any more by the waters of a flood; neither shall they any more be a flood to destroy the earth... And it shall come to pass, when I bring a cloud over the earth, that the bow shall be seen in the cloud: And I will remember my covenant, which is between me and you and every living creature of all flesh; and the waters shall no more become a flood to destroy all flesh." Genesis 9:11, 14, 15

TWO: Sodom and Gomorrah (Genesis Chapter 18 and 19)

Sodom and Gomorrah were two of five cities in the plentifully watered and very fertile plain of the River Jordan. We are first introduced to these cities in Genesis 13 when Lot and Abram parted ways and Lot chose to live in the plain of Jordan.

"And Abram said unto Lot, Let there be no strife, I pray thee, between me and thee, and between my herdmen and thy herdmen, for we be brethren. Is not the whole land before thee? Separate thyself, I pray thee, from me: if thou wilt take the left hand, then I will go to the right, or if thou depart to the right hand, then I will go to the left. And Lot lifted up his eyes, and beheld all the plain of Jordan, that it was well watered every where, before the Lord destroyed Sodom and Gomorrah, even as the garden of the Lord, like the land of Egypt, as thou comest unto Zoar. Then Lot chose him all the plain of Jordan, and Lot journeyed east: and they separated themselves the one from the other. Abram dwelled in the land of Canaan, and Lot dwelled in the cities of the plain, and pitched his tent toward Sodom." Genesis 13:8-12.

Right away we are told about the character of the inhabitants of Sodom.

"But the men of Sodom were wicked and sinners before the Lord exceedingly." Genesis 13:13.

The five cities of the plain are mentioned in Genesis 14 when they were collectively under a military attack by four kings led by the king of Elam. The battle took place in the very fertile plain of Jordan in an area called the Vale of Siddim (which is now the salt sea).

"And it came to pass in the days of Amraphel king of Shinar, Arioch king of Ellasar, Chedorlaomer king of Elam, and Tidal king of nations; That these made war with Bera king of Sodom, and with Birsha king of Gomorrah, Shinab king of Admah, and Shemeber king of Zeboiim, and the king of Bela, which is Zoar. All these were joined together in the vale of Siddim, which is the salt sea." Genesis 14:1-3

Some very important information is given in verse 10.

"And the vale of Siddim was full of slimepits; and the kings of Sodom and Gomorrah fled, and fell there; and they that remained fled to the mountain." Genesis 14:10.

The vale of Siddim, the beautiful fertile valley surrounding the cities of the plain **was full of slime pits.** The slime pits oozed out asphalt from beneath the earth's surface. Obviously this was an area where immense amounts of trees had been buried during the Flood resulting in the formation of petroleum products.

The cities of the plain were sitting, as it were, on a natural "time-bomb" and they neither knew nor cared.

God's protection, God's blessings, God's mercy sustained the cities of the plain maintaining life and fertility. But their probation was fast closing.

In Genesis 18, Abraham was visited by three Heavenly Beings. One was the Son of God! Abraham addressed Him as LORD meaning Jehovah.

The LORD announced to Abraham and Sarah that the son of promise would be born a year later and then He announced the fact that probation for the cities of the plain was rapidly closing. The LORD revealed to Abraham that Divine Judgment would be pronounced and executed upon Sodom and Gomorrah and their neighboring cities.

The actual description of the execution of Divine Judgment is written down in Genesis 19:23-29.

"The sun was risen upon the earth when Lot entered into Zoar. Then the Lord rained upon Sodom and upon Gomorrah brimstone and fire from the Lord out of heaven; And he overthrew those cities, and all the plain, and all the inhabitants of the cities, and that which grew upon the ground. But his wife looked back from behind him, and she became a pillar of salt. And Abraham gat up early in the morning to the place where he stood before the Lord: And he looked toward Sodom and Gomorrah, and toward all the land of the plain, and beheld, and, lo, the smoke of the country went up as the smoke of a furnace. And it came to pass, when God destroyed the cities of the plain, that God remembered Abraham, and sent Lot out of the midst of the overthrow, when he overthrew the cities in the which Lot dwelt." Genesis 19:23-29.

Again the language is clear: it says that the LORD rained upon Sodom and Gomorrah brimstone and fire from the LORD out of heaven. He destroyed, He overthrew those cities!

Does scripture give us the correct interpretation of such language in terms of the mechanism by which those cities were destroyed?

Yes!

Our first evidence comes from Deuteronomy chapter 29 where Moses reminded the Israelites of God's covenant with them, the blessings of obedience and the curses of disobedience which are listed in Chapter 28.

He particularly mentioned in Deut. 29:18, 19 the sins of idolatry, false worship and boastful defiance.

Moses then clearly outlined the punishments which would befall the people and their land in Deuteronomy 29: 20-29. Let us consider verse 23.

"And that the whole land thereof is brimstone, and salt, and burning, that it is not sown, nor beareth, nor any grass growth therein, like the overthrow of Sodom, and Gomorrah, Admah, and Zeboim, which the Lord overthrew in his anger, and in his wrath." Deut. 29:23.

Here Moses clearly stated that God would do to them like He did to Sodom and Gomorrah, Admah and Zeboim. He would overthrow the land with fire and brimstone and salt. This would be the result of God's anger kindled against the land.

"And the anger of the Lord was kindled against this land, to bring upon it all the curses that are written in this book." Deut. 29:27.

But over in Deuteronomy 31:16-18 God explained the mechanism of wrath.

"And the Lord said unto Moses, Behold, thou shalt sleep with thy fathers, and this people will rise up, and go a whoring after the gods of the strangers of the land, whither they go to be among them, and will forsake me, and break my covenant which I have made with them. Then my anger shall be kindled against them in that day, and I will forsake them and I will hide my face from them, and they shall be devoured, and many evils and troubles shall befall them; so that they will say in that day, are not these evils come upon us, because our God is not among us? And I will surely hide my face in that day for all the evils which they shall have wrought, in that they are turned unto other gods." Deut. 31:16-18.

Therefore the overthrow of the land with fire and brimstone and salt would be the result of God forsaking them and hiding His face from them.

Obviously then the sins of the cities of the plain reached that point where the inhabitants passed the limits of divine forbearance, their minds were irreversibly fixed against God. They did not want God and God withdrew from them. They did not realize that God's Spirit through His angels was holding in check the sin-perverted forces of nature around them. When God let go there was nothing to prevent the fiery explosion which destroyed them.

This is further confirmed in Amos 4:9-11, where God rehearsed some of the curses with which Israel was smitten. He told them:

"I have overthrown some of you, as God overthrew Sodom and Gomorrah, and ye were as a firebrand plucked out of the burning: yet have ye not returned unto me, saith the Lord." Amos 4:11.

It is clear then that the mechanism of Sodom's overthrow was the same mechanism stated in Deuteronomy 31:16-18. Our third confirmatory evidence is written down in Hosea 11:7, 8.

"And my people are bent to backsliding from me: though they called them to the most High, none at all would exalt him. How shall I give thee up, Ephraim? How shall I deliver thee, Israel? How shall I make thee as Admah? How shall I see thee as Zeboim? Mine heart is turned within me, my repentings are kindled together." Hosea 11:7, 8.

God asked Ephraim and Israel: "How shall I give thee up? How shall I deliver thee?" And in giving Israel up He would be making her as Admah and Zeboim, the cities of the plain. Therefore the cities of the plain were "given up" or "delivered up". And they were **delivered to trouble and commotion.**

"Wherefore the wrath of the Lord was upon Judah and Jerusalem, and he hath delivered them to trouble, to astonishment, and to hissing, as ye see with your eyes. For, lo, our fathers have fallen by the sword, and ours sons and our daughters and our wives are in captivity for this." 2 Chron. 29:8, 9.

In Romans 1, Paul explains that God's wrath is exercised when He gives up those who reject His mercy. (See Romans 1:18, 24, 26, 28). Sodom and Gomorrah and the cities of the plain were given up by God. He hid His face from them. He forsook them. He withdrew his protection and they were consumed by a fiery explosion.

One last point must be clarified.

The fire with brimstone is described as falling from God out of heaven. We met a similar term in Job 1:16 when it is said that "the fire of God is fallen from heaven…" But such fire resulted when God handed over Job's possessions to Satan, Job 1:12. In other words the "fire of God fallen from heaven" is caused by sin's separation from God.

Made in the USA
Charleston, SC
25 February 2016